GRAPHIC LIBRARY™

STEM ADVENTURES

THE TERRIFIC TALE OF
TELEVISION TECHNOLOGY

MAX AXIOM
STEM ADVENTURES

by Tammy Enz

illustrated by Pop Art Properties

Consultant:
Akbar M. Sayeed, PhD
Professor
Department of Electrical and Computer Engineering
College of Engineering
University of Wisconsin-Madison

CAPSTONE PRESS
a capstone imprint

Graphic Library is published by Capstone Press,
1710 Roe Crest Drive, North Mankato, Minnesota 56003
www.capstonepub.com

Library of Congress Cataloging-in-Publication Data
Enz, Tammy.
The terrific tale of television technology : Max Axiom STEM adventures / by Tammy Enz;
illustrated by Pop Art Properties.
pages cm.—(Graphic library. STEM adventures.)
Summary: "In graphic novel format, follow Max Axiom as he explains how television
technology works"—Provided by publisher.
Audience: Grade 4 to 6.
Includes bibliographical references and index.
ISBN 978-1-4765-0138-3 (library binding)
ISBN 978-1-4765-3458-9 (paperback)
ISBN 978-1-4765-3454-1 (eBook PDF)
1. Television—Juvenile literature. 2. Television—Comic books, strips, etc. 3. Graphic
novels. I. Pop Art Properties, illustrator. II. Title.
TK6640.E59 2014
621.388—dc23   2013003115

Designer
Ted Williams

Cover Artist
Marcelo Baez

Media Researcher
Wanda Winch

Production Specialist
Eric Manske

Editor
Christopher L. Harbo

Photo Credits: Shutterstock: Pupes, 23

Printed in the United States of America in Stevens Point, Wisconsin.
032013   007227WZF13

TABLE of CONTENTS

SECTION 1

CREATING THE CONTENT----------4

SECTION 2

SENDING THE SIGNAL-------------10

SECTION 3

DECODING THE DRAMA------------18

SECTION 4

BEYOND THE BASICS ------------24

More about TV Technology 28
Critical Thinking Using the Common Core 29
Glossary 30
Read More 31
Internet Sites 31
Index 32

SECTION 1 CREATING THE CONTENT

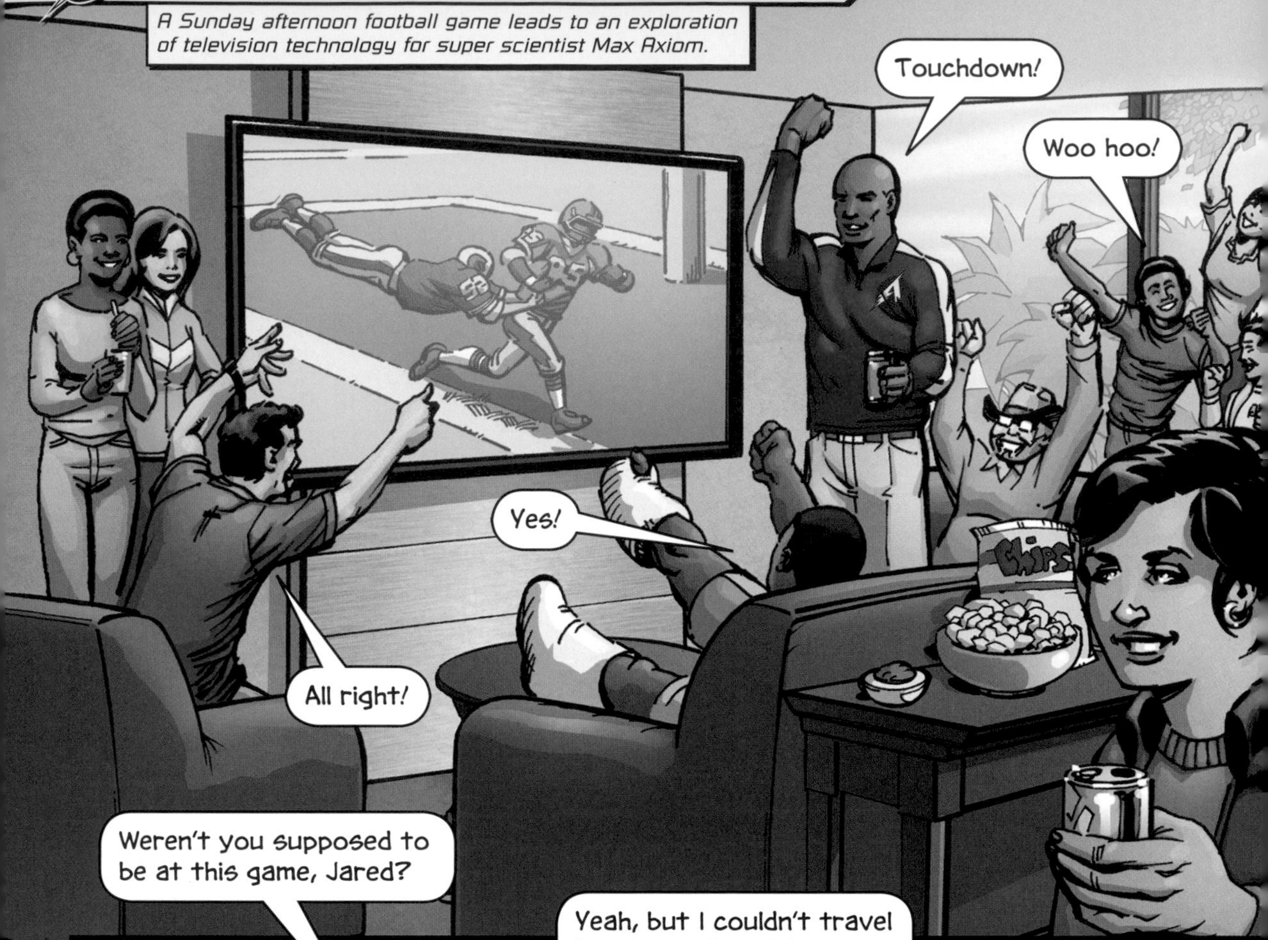
A Sunday afternoon football game leads to an exploration of television technology for super scientist Max Axiom.
Touchdown!
Woo hoo!
Yes!
All right!
Weren't you supposed to be at this game, Jared?

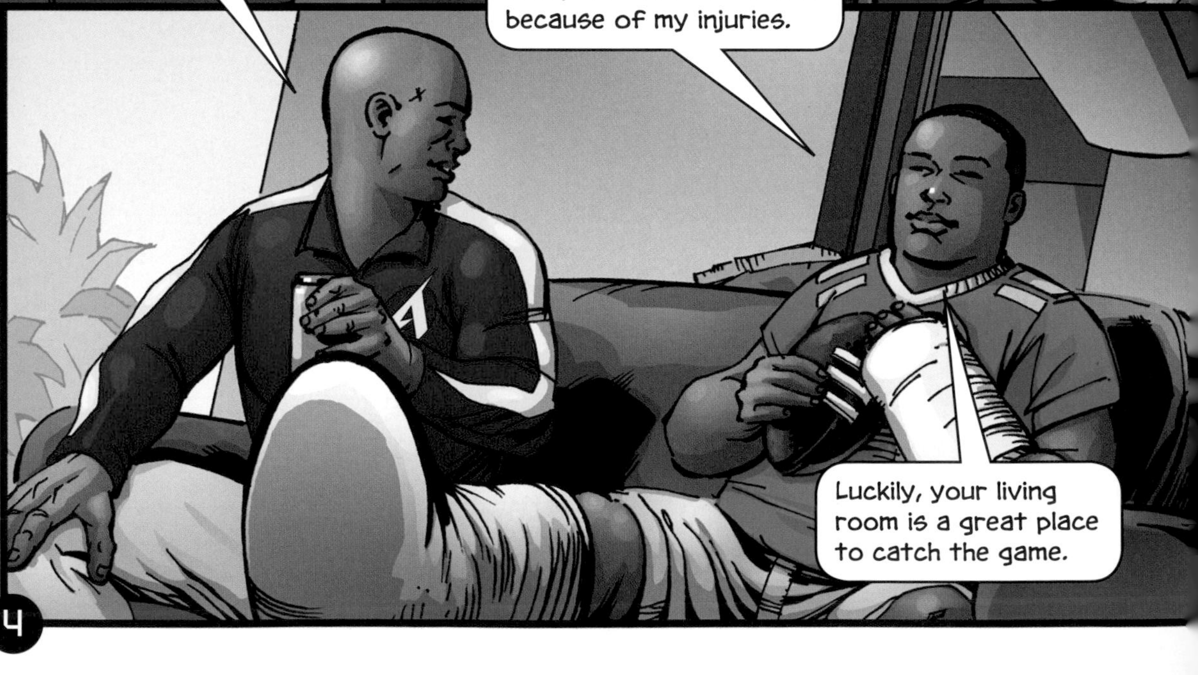
Yeah, but I couldn't travel because of my injuries.
Luckily, your living room is a great place to catch the game.

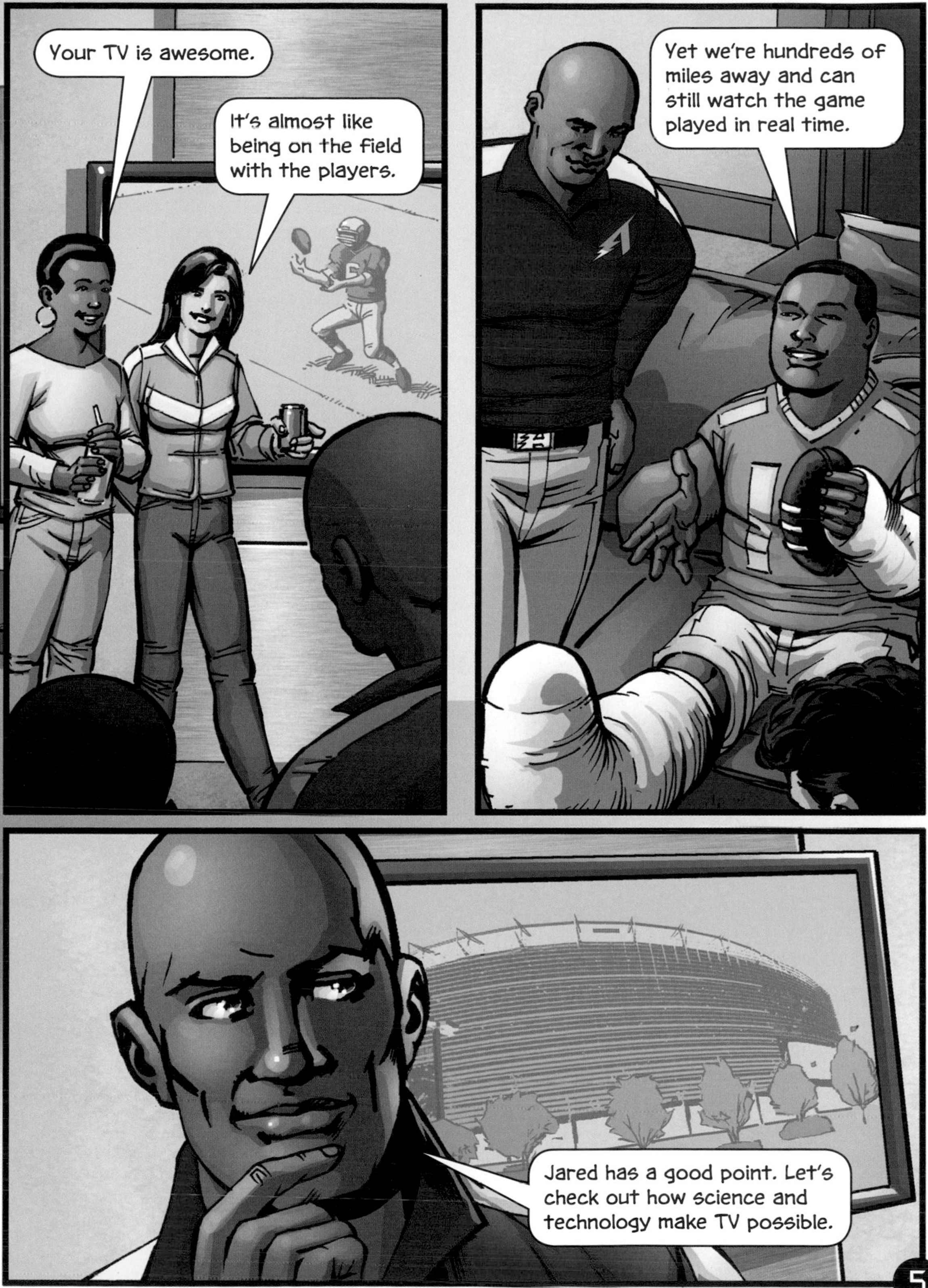
Your TV is awesome.
It's almost like being on the field with the players.
Yet we're hundreds of miles away and can still watch the game played in real time.
Jared has a good point. Let's check out how science and technology make TV possible.

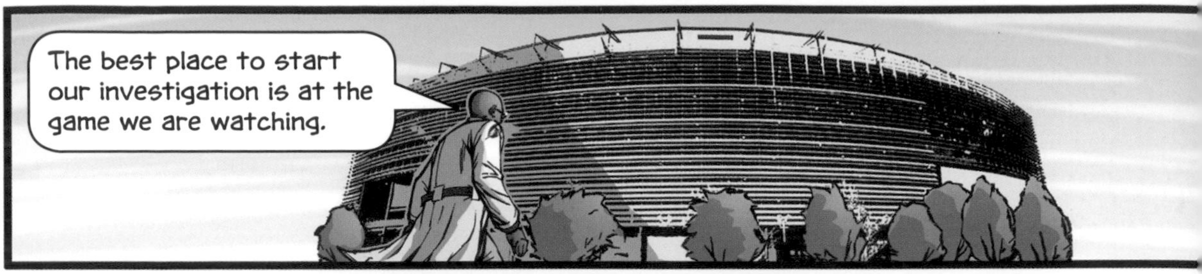
The best place to start our investigation is at the game we are watching.

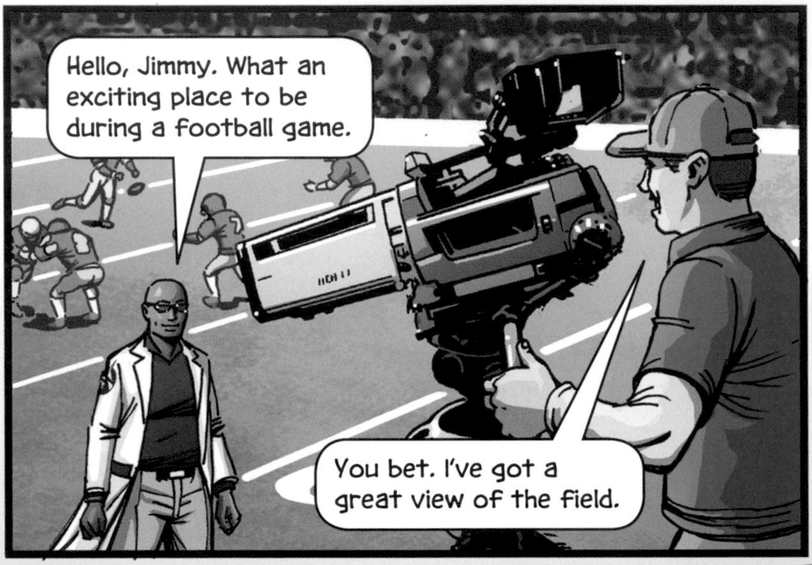
Hello, Jimmy. What an exciting place to be during a football game.
You bet. I've got a great view of the field.

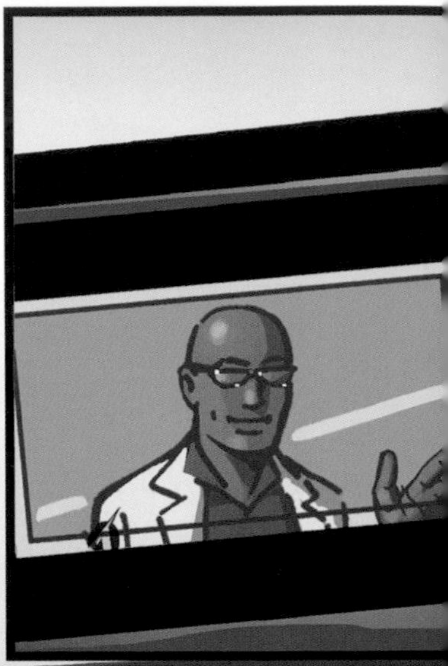

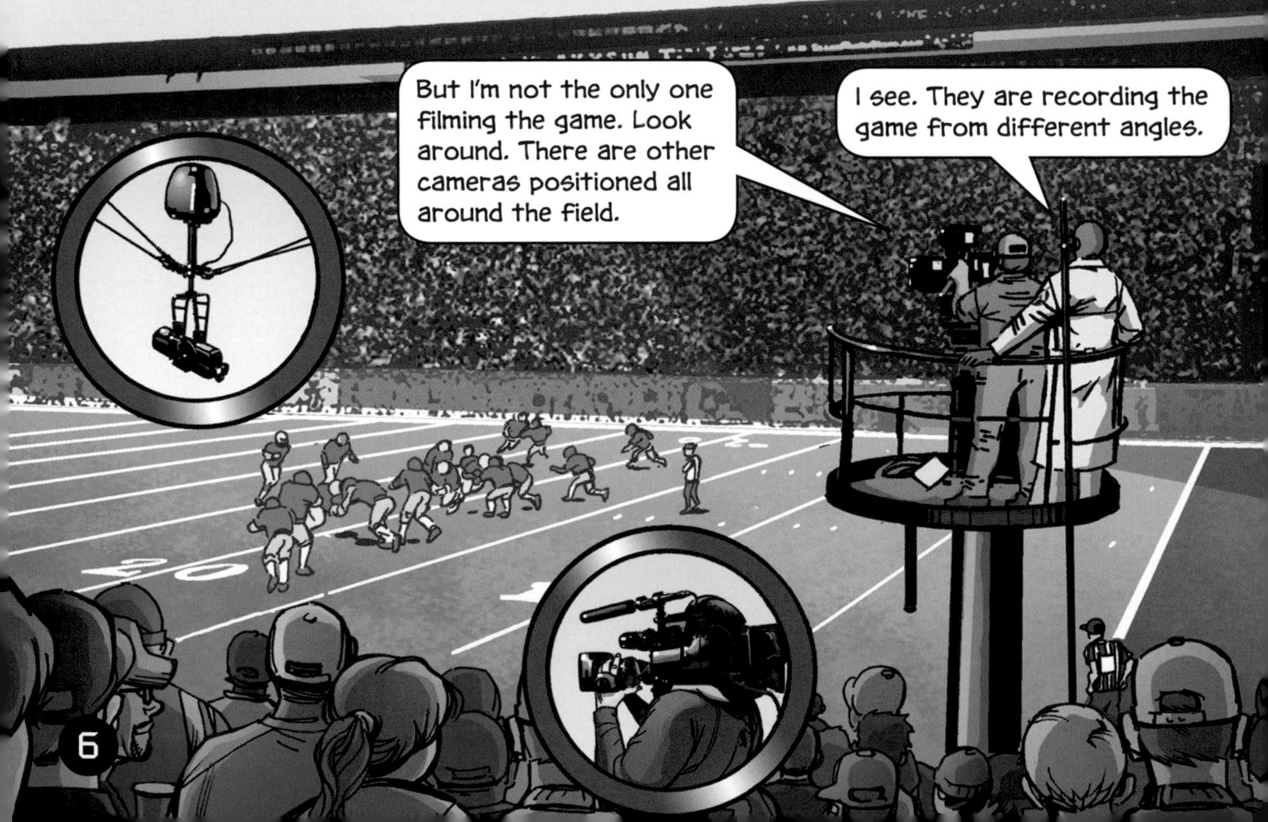
But I'm not the only one filming the game. Look around. There are other cameras positioned all around the field.
I see. They are recording the game from different angles.

Our cameras capture each play. They turn the pictures into video signals that are sent to a broadcasting center.

At the same time, microphones capture the sounds that go with the picture. These sounds are sent alongside the picture information as a separate audio signal.

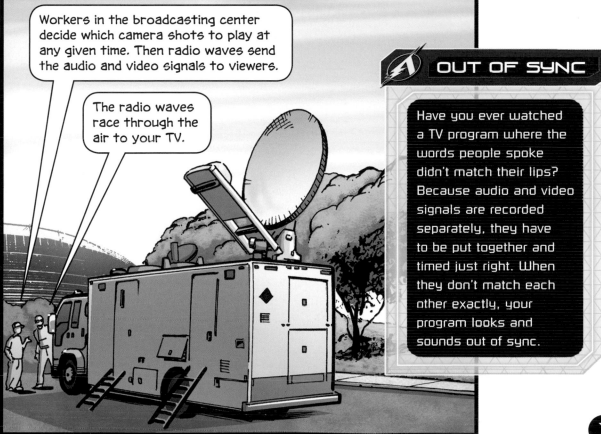

Workers in the broadcasting center decide which camera shots to play at any given time. Then radio waves send the audio and video signals to viewers.

The radio waves race through the air to your TV.

OUT OF SYNC

Have you ever watched a TV program where the words people spoke didn't match their lips? Because audio and video signals are recorded separately, they have to be put together and timed just right. When they don't match each other exactly, your program looks and sounds out of sync.

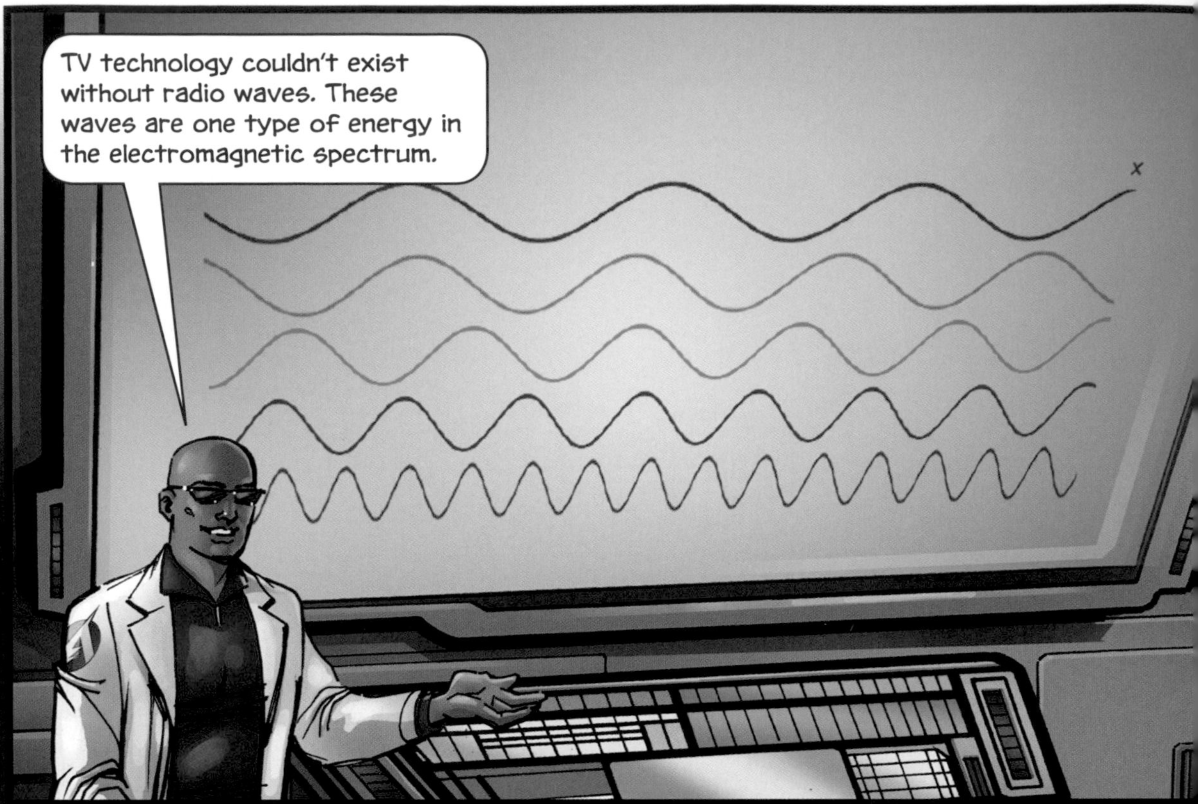
TV technology couldn't exist without radio waves. These waves are one type of energy in the electromagnetic spectrum.

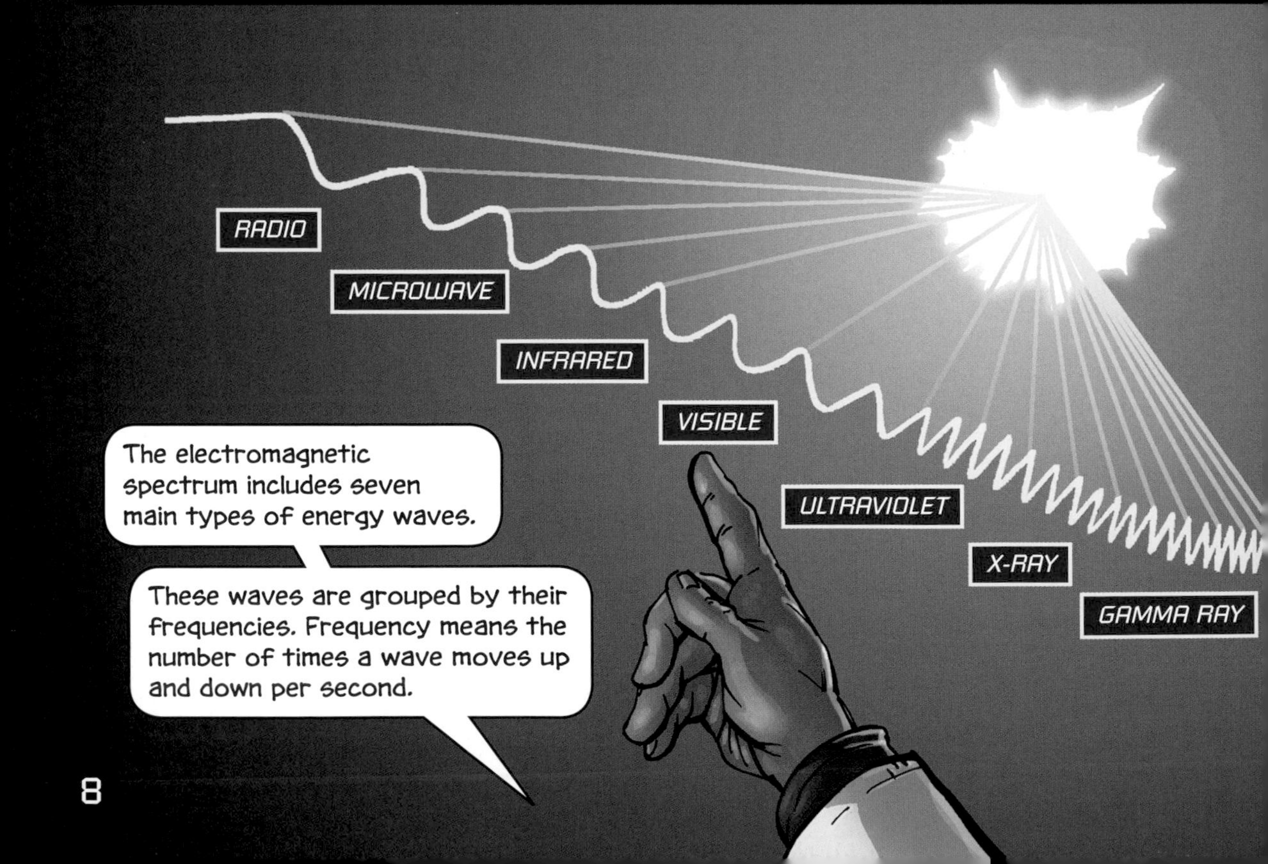
RADIO
MICROWAVE
INFRARED
VISIBLE
ULTRAVIOLET
X-RAY
GAMMA RAY
The electromagnetic spectrum includes seven main types of energy waves.
These waves are grouped by their frequencies. Frequency means the number of times a wave moves up and down per second.

ONE SECOND

20 HERTZ

Frequency is measured with a unit called hertz. If a wave moves up and down 20 times in a second, we call that 20 hertz.

Radio waves have fairly low frequencies. They range from 50 to 1,000 million hertz.

TV signals aren't the only things carried by radio raves. Radio broadcasts, walkie-talkie and cell phone conversations, and wireless Internet signals also use radio waves.

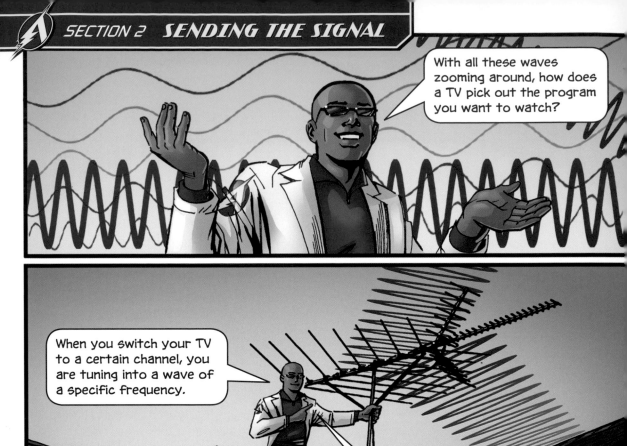

With all these waves zooming around, how does a TV pick out the program you want to watch?

When you switch your TV to a certain channel, you are tuning into a wave of a specific frequency.

On some homes, a TV antenna amplifies the frequency you want and reduces other frequencies.

But not all waves can reach these TV antennas without help. TV signals are direct waves. They travel in a straight line. They cannot bend around the curve of Earth's surface.

For waves to travel around Earth, large antennas called relay towers must catch them. They redirect the waves around Earth's curved surface.

TV signals also get weaker as they travel. Weak signals may not reach your antenna. Also, large objects like mountains and tall buildings sometimes block signals.

In these cases, TV signals need other ways to reach your home. Cable TV and satellite TV are perfect examples.

Let's see how they work.

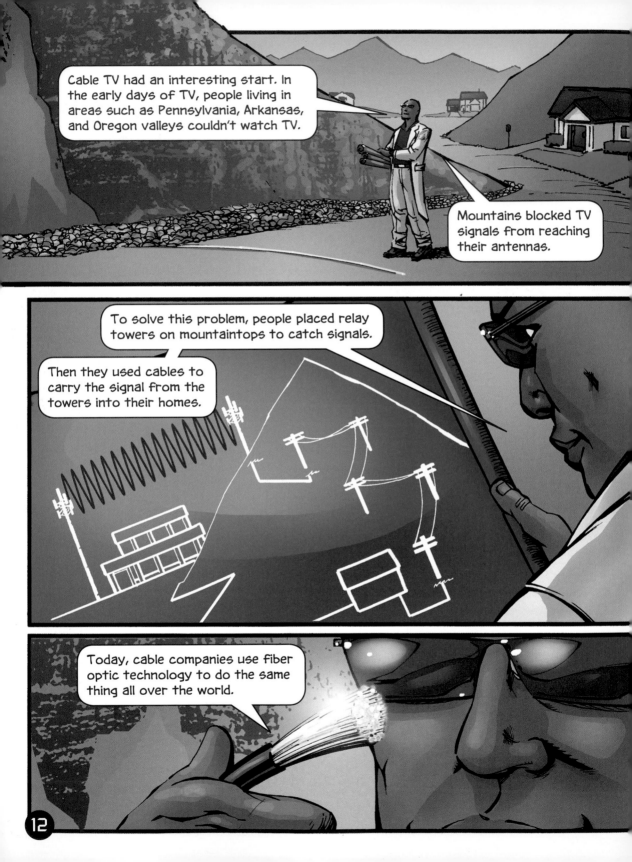

Cable TV had an interesting start. In the early days of TV, people living in areas such as Pennsylvania, Arkansas, and Oregon valleys couldn't watch TV.

Mountains blocked TV signals from reaching their antennas.

To solve this problem, people placed relay towers on mountaintops to catch signals.

Then they used cables to carry the signal from the towers into their homes.

Today, cable companies use fiber optic technology to do the same thing all over the world.

Cable companies collect broadcast signals and change them into beams of light. The light beams travel through underground cables and into people's homes.

Cable signals allow TV viewers to watch hundreds of different channels.

Hi, Rosa. What are you working on?

I'm installing a cable TV system. The signal in the cable leading up to this box is in code.

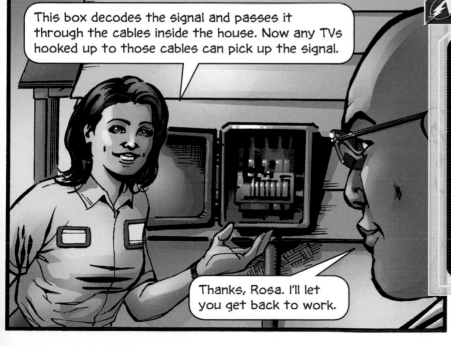

This box decodes the signal and passes it through the cables inside the house. Now any TVs hooked up to those cables can pick up the signal.

Thanks, Rosa. I'll let you get back to work.

A FIBER OPTICS

Fiber optic cables are used for telephone lines, cable TV, and the Internet. These cables are made of strands of pure glass as thin as a human hair. They can carry information over long distances.

Satellite TV is another way people can watch a huge variety of channels.

Satellite TV works a lot like regular broadcast and cable TV. It uses radio waves to carry TV signals.

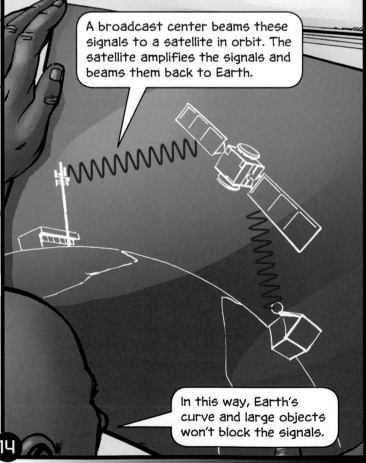

A broadcast center beams these signals to a satellite in orbit. The satellite amplifies the signals and beams them back to Earth.

In this way, Earth's curve and large objects won't block the signals.

The key to satellite signals are antennas called satellite dishes. They send and collect these signals.

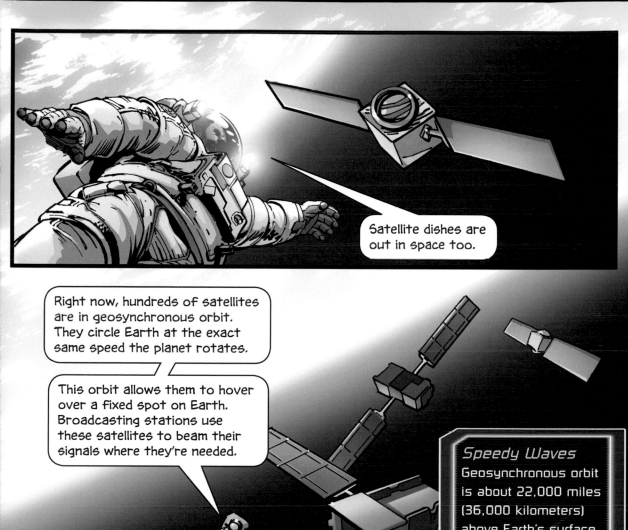

Satellite dishes are out in space too.

Right now, hundreds of satellites are in geosynchronous orbit. They circle Earth at the exact same speed the planet rotates.

This orbit allows them to hover over a fixed spot on Earth. Broadcasting stations use these satellites to beam their signals where they're needed.

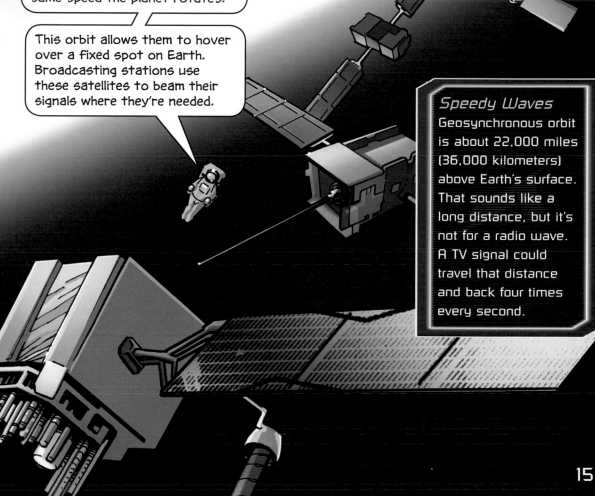

Speedy Waves
Geosynchronous orbit is about 22,000 miles (36,000 kilometers) above Earth's surface. That sounds like a long distance, but it's not for a radio wave. A TV signal could travel that distance and back four times every second.

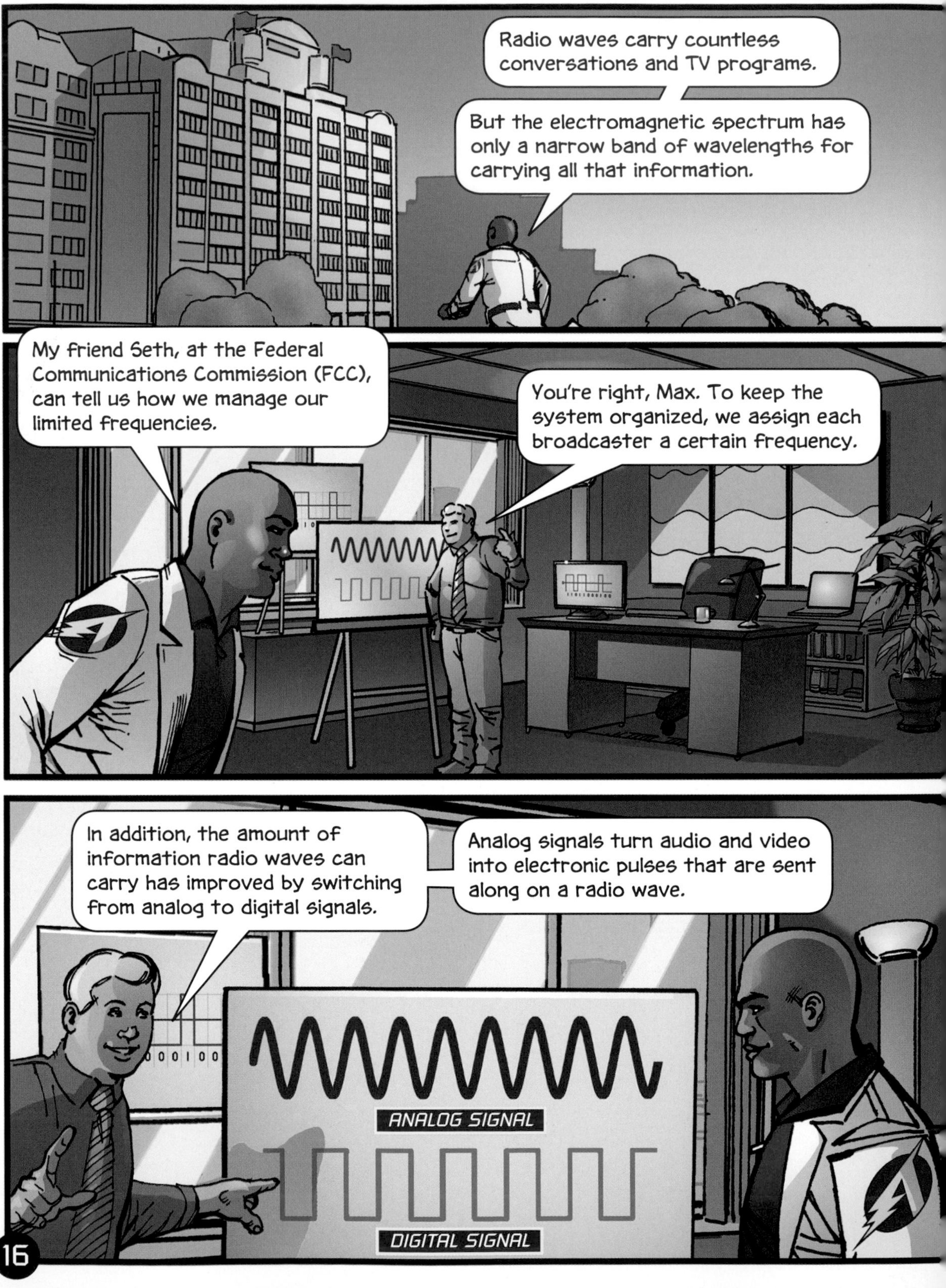
Radio waves carry countless conversations and TV programs.
But the electromagnetic spectrum has only a narrow band of wavelengths for carrying all that information.
My friend Seth, at the Federal Communications Commission (FCC), can tell us how we manage our limited frequencies.
You're right, Max. To keep the system organized, we assign each broadcaster a certain frequency.
In addition, the amount of information radio waves can carry has improved by switching from analog to digital signals.
Analog signals turn audio and video into electronic pulses that are sent along on a radio wave.
ANALOG SIGNAL
DIGITAL SIGNAL

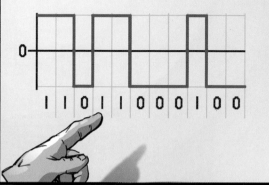

But digital processes break signals into a binary format. Every sound and picture is represented by a different series of 1s and 0s.

I I 0 I I 0 0 0 I 0 0

The 0s and 1s are sent along on a radio wave. Then your TV puts the numbers back together into their original meanings.

Digital signals allow broadcasters to include surround sound, subtitles, and different languages in TV programs.

Thanks, Seth. Good to know you're keeping an eye on our frequencies.

⚡ MAKING THE SWITCH

After June 12, 2009, the U.S. Congress required all major broadcasters to use digital signals. Before this date, many broadcasters sent out both digital and analog signals.

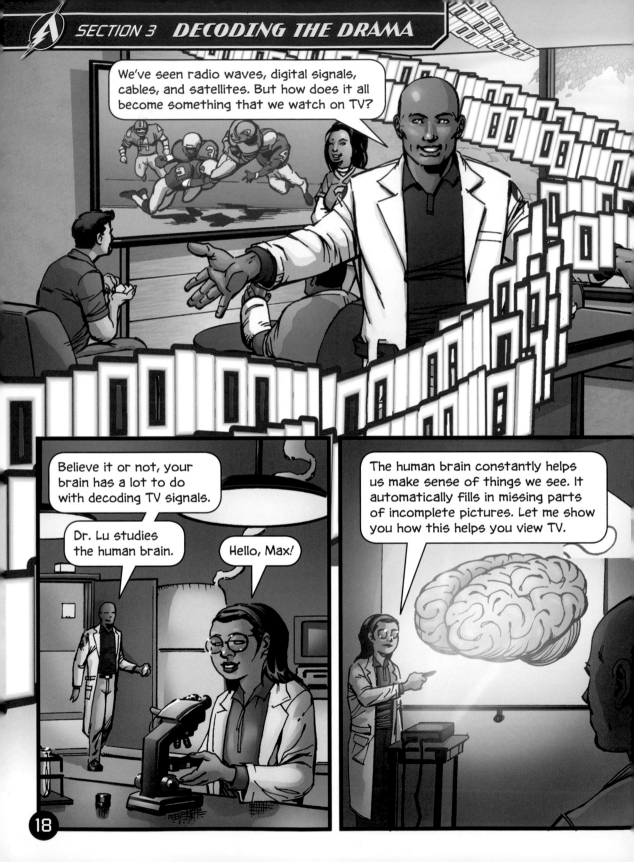

We've seen radio waves, digital signals, cables, and satellites. But how does it all become something that we watch on TV?

Believe it or not, your brain has a lot to do with decoding TV signals.

Dr. Lu studies the human brain.

Hello, Max!

The human brain constantly helps us make sense of things we see. It automatically fills in missing parts of incomplete pictures. Let me show you how this helps you view TV.

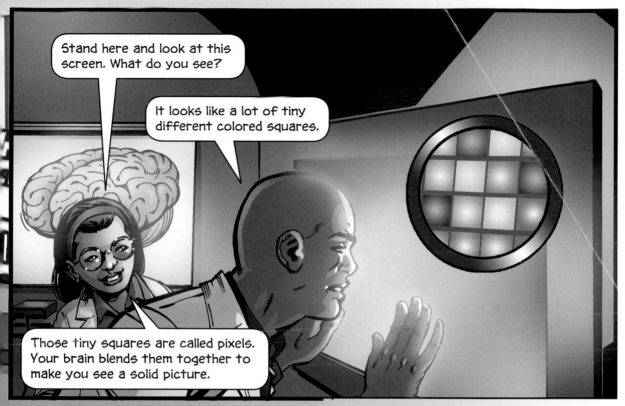

Stand here and look at this screen. What do you see?

It looks like a lot of tiny different colored squares.

Those tiny squares are called pixels. Your brain blends them together to make you see a solid picture.

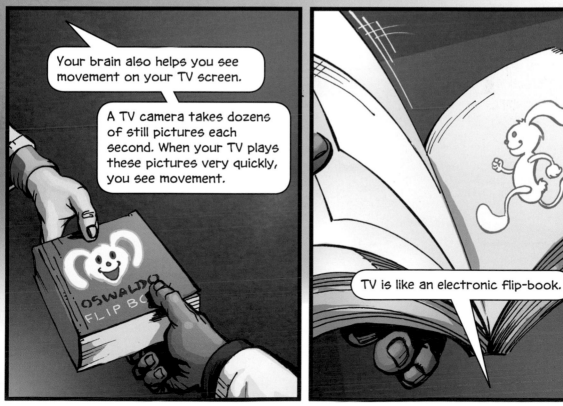

Your brain also helps you see movement on your TV screen.

A TV camera takes dozens of still pictures each second. When your TV plays these pictures very quickly, you see movement.

OSWALDO FLIP BOOK

TV is like an electronic flip-book.

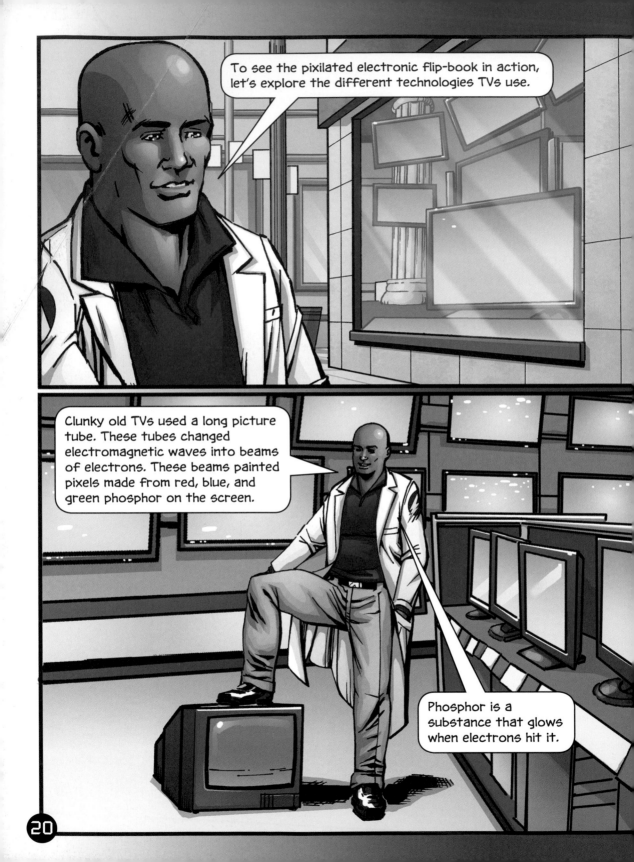

To see the pixilated electronic flip-book in action, let's explore the different technologies TVs use.

Clunky old TVs used a long picture tube. These tubes changed electromagnetic waves into beams of electrons. These beams painted pixels made from red, blue, and green phosphor on the screen.

Phosphor is a substance that glows when electrons hit it.

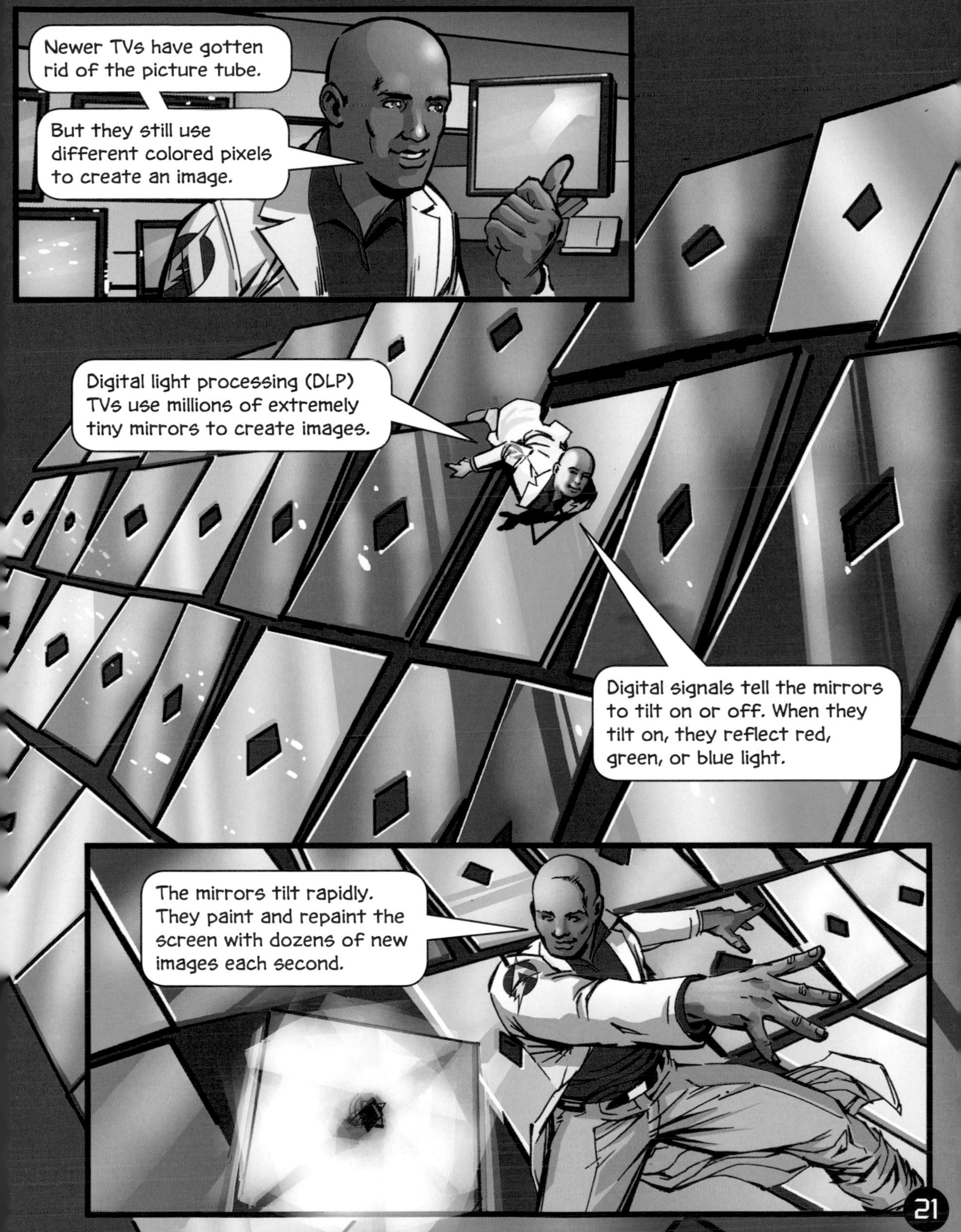
Newer TVs have gotten rid of the picture tube.
But they still use different colored pixels to create an image.
Digital light processing (DLP) TVs use millions of extremely tiny mirrors to create images.
Digital signals tell the mirrors to tilt on or off. When they tilt on, they reflect red, green, or blue light.
The mirrors tilt rapidly. They paint and repaint the screen with dozens of new images each second.

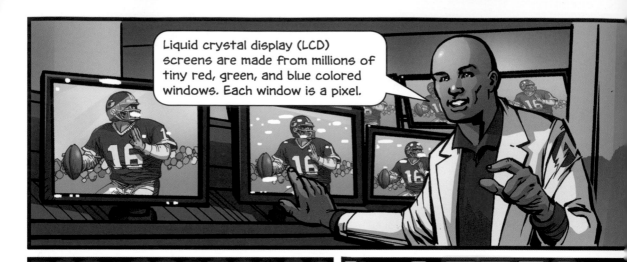

Liquid crystal display (LCD) screens are made from millions of tiny red, green, and blue colored windows. Each window is a pixel.

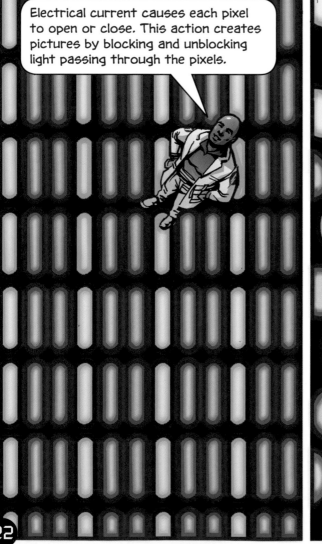

Electrical current causes each pixel to open or close. This action creates pictures by blocking and unblocking light passing through the pixels.

Light emitting diode (LED) screens use microscopic lightbulbs. These bulbs switch on or off electronically to make a picture.

A plasma screen is similar to an LCD, except each pixel is a microscopic fluorescent lamp glowing with plasma.

Plasma is cool stuff. It is a very hot form of gas in which the atoms have been blown apart. Plasma causes fluorescent lightbulbs and neon signs to glow.

HIGH-DEFINITION

High-definition TV (HDTV) models produce the highest quality pictures of all digital TVs. They have much higher resolution by using more pixels than other TVs. They also have faster frame rates. They "repaint" the picture on the screen twice as fast as standard TV sets.

One of my favorite pieces of TV technology is the remote control. It allows me to change channels and volume on my TV without ever getting out of my chair.

Remote control devices also use part of the electromagnetic spectrum to operate.

Electromagnetic Spectrum

Microwave | Sub-mm | Infrared | Ultraviolet | X-ray | Gamma ray

But they use infrared light instead of radio waves.

When you press a button on a remote, it emits a stream of infrared light.

This light is actually a code sent as a series of pulses.

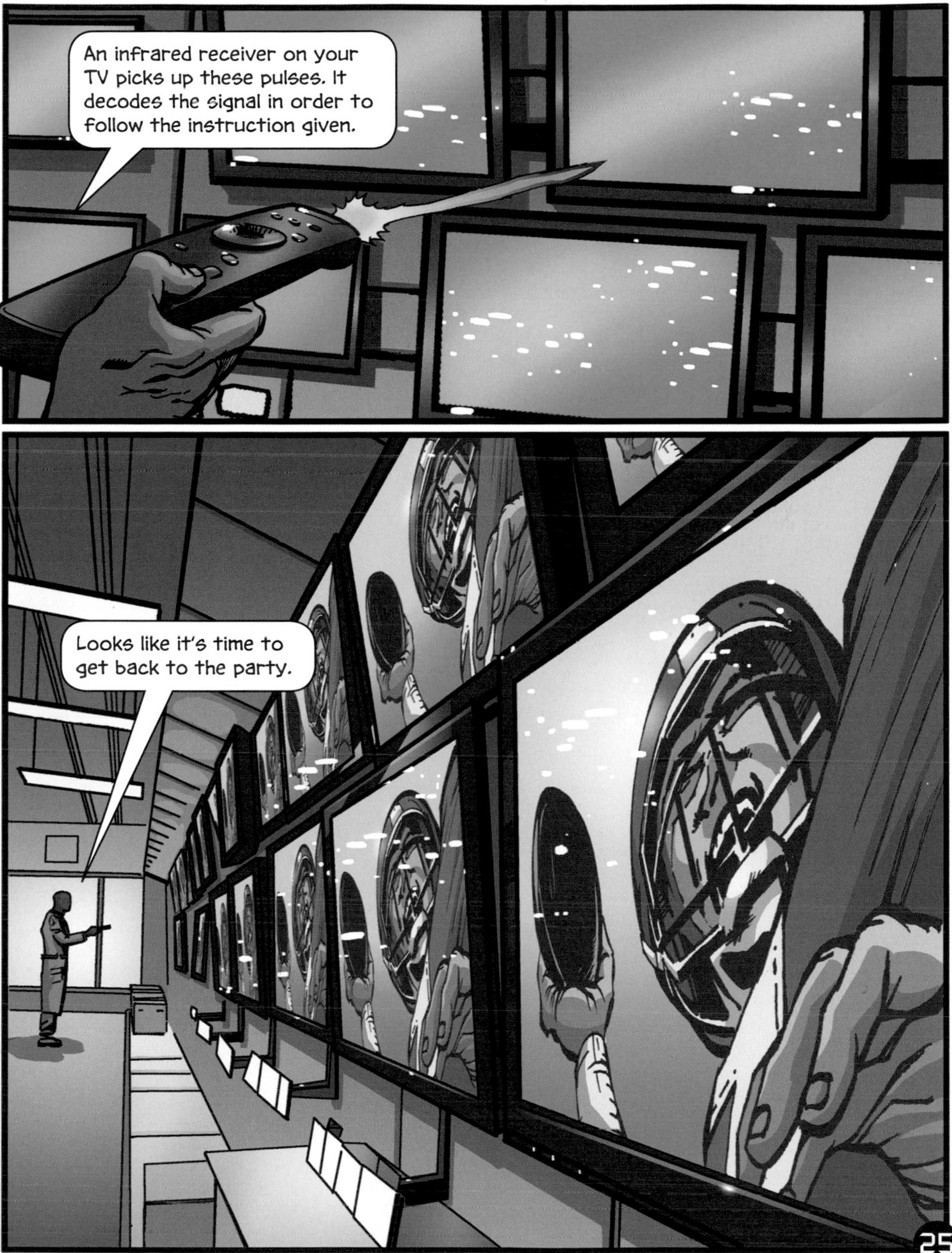
An infrared receiver on your TV picks up these pulses. It decodes the signal in order to follow the instruction given.
Looks like it's time to get back to the party.

A lot of technology goes into watching a game. TV signals travel to our homes at the speed of light.

The TV screen turns those signals into pictures made up of millions of tiny pixels.

TWELVE SECONDS LEFT ... JACKSON HAS THE BALL ...

The pixels quickly change color so we see movement on the screen.

HE CUTS LEFT ... SPINS ... BREAKS A TACKLE ...

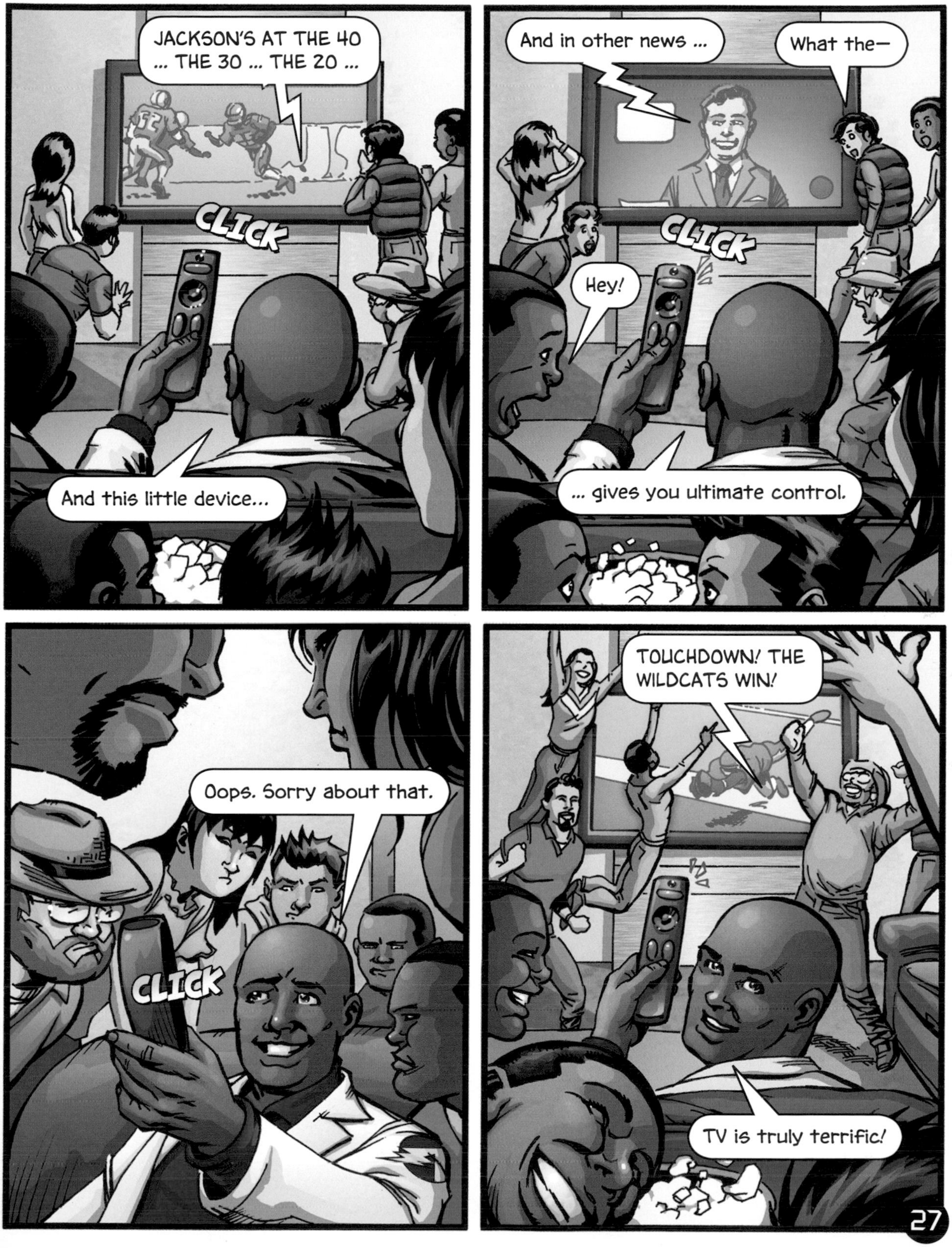
JACKSON'S AT THE 40 ... THE 30 ... THE 20 ...
CLICK
And this little device...
And in other news ...
What the—
CLICK
Hey!
... gives you ultimate control.
Oops. Sorry about that.
CLICK
TOUCHDOWN! THE WILDCATS WIN!
TV is truly terrific!

MORE ABOUT TV TECHNOLOGY

German scientist Heinrich Hertz was the first person to send and receive radio waves. Between 1885 and 1889, he measured the length and speed of radio waves in his lab. His research led to the use of radio waves in many modern communication devices.

Scientists invented the first remote controls for use during World War I (1914–1918) and World War II (1939–1945). These devices were used to ram unmanned boats into enemy ships and to detonate bombs. The first wireless remote control for a TV came along in 1955. It was called the Zenith "Flash-Matic."

Many inventors had a hand in the components that make TV possible. Russian-born American engineer Vladimir Zworykin patented a TV transmission tube called an iconoscope in 1923. One year later, he patented a TV receiver called a kinescope. Meanwhile, Philo Farnsworth invented the first all-electronic television system in 1927. The work of both inventors led to TV becoming a modern fixture for entertainment and education in the home.

More than 1,000 communications satellites orbit Earth. We rely on them for radio, TV, and cell phone service. But what happens when old communications satellites stop working? Most are blasted farther into orbit, where they continue to circle Earth as space junk. Many of these junked satellites end up about 186 miles (300 km) from their original orbits. At this distance, they can't collide with working satellites.

1. What is the difference between an analog signal and a digital signal? How is the switch from analog to digital changing the way we watch TV? (Key Ideas and Details)

2. Max says TV signals are direct waves. How do the illustrations at the bottom of page 10 and the top of page 11 help you understand what Max means by *direct waves*? (Craft and Structure)

3. List at least five devices your family owns that use radio waves. Which of these devices would be most difficult for your family to live without? Explain why. (Integration of Knowledge and Ideas)

MORE ABOUT

SUPER SCIENTIST

Real name: Maxwell J. Axiom
Hometown: Seattle, Washington
Height: 6' 1"   Weight: 192 lbs
Eyes: Brown   Hair: None

Super capabilities: Super intelligence; able to shrink to the size of an atom; sunglasses give x-ray vision; lab coat allows for travel through time and space.

Origin: Since birth, Max Axiom seemed destined for greatness. His mother, a marine biologist, taught her son about the mysteries of the sea. His father, a nuclear physicist and volunteer park ranger, schooled Max on the wonders of earth and sky.

One day on a wilderness hike, a megacharged lightning bolt struck Max with blinding fury. When he awoke, Max discovered a newfound energy and set out to learn as much about science as possible. He traveled the globe earning degrees in every aspect of the field. Upon his return, he was ready to share his knowledge and new identity with the world. He had become Max Axiom, Super Scientist.

Glossary

amplify (AM-pli-fye)—to make something louder or stronger

antenna (an-TEN-uh)—a wire or dish that sends or receives radio waves

electromagnetic spectrum (i-lek-troh-mag-NET-ik SPEK-truhm)—the wide range of energy given off by the sun

engineer (en-juh-NEER)—someone trained to design and build machines, vehicles, bridges, roads, or other structures

frequency (FREE-kwuhn-see)—the number of sound waves that pass a location in a certain amount of time

hertz (HURTS)—a unit for measuring the frequency of sound wave vibrations; one hertz equals one sound wave per second

infrared light (IN-fruh-red LITE)—invisible light waves just longer than red light waves on the electromagnetic spectrum

phosphor (FAHS-for)—a material that glows when exposed to light or other forms of energy

pixel (PIKS-uhl)—one of the tiny dots on a TV screen that makes up the visual image

radio wave (RAY-dee-oh WAYV)—a type of electromagnetic wave; electromagnetic waves are caused by electricity and magnetism

satellite (SAT-uh-lite)—a spacecraft used to send signals and information from one place to another

READ MORE

Bryant, Jill. *Technology Mysteries Revealed.* Mysteries Revealed. New York: Crabtree Pub. Company, 2010.

Chmielewski, Gary T. *How Did That Get to My House?: Television.* Community Connections. Ann Arbor, Mich.: Cherry Lake Pub., 2010.

Enz, Tammy. *Zoom It: Invent New Machines That Move.* Invent It. Mankato, Minn.: Capstone Press, 2012.

Petrie, Kristin. *Televisions.* Everyday Inventions. Edina, Minn.: ABDO, 2009.

Spilsbury, Richard, and Louise. *The Television.* Tales of Invention. Chicago: Heinemann Library, 2012.

INTERNET SITES

FactHound offers a safe, fun way to find Internet sites related to this book. All sites on FactHound have been researched by our staff.

Here's all you do:

Visit *www.facthound.com*

Type in this code: 9781476501383

antennas, 10, 11, 12, 14

blocked signals, 11, 12, 14
broadcast centers, 7, 14, 15
broadcasters, 16, 17

cable TV, 11, 12–13, 14, 18
channels, 10, 13, 14, 24

digital light processing (DLP) TVs, 21
direct waves, 10

electromagnetic spectrum, 8, 16, 24

Farnsworth, Philo, 28
Federal Communications Commission (FCC), 16
fiber optics, 12, 13
frequencies, 8–9, 10, 16, 17

hertz, 9
Hertz, Heinrich, 28
high-definition TV (HDTV), 23

infrared light, 24
infrared receiver, 25

light emitting diode (LED) TVs, 22
liquid crystal display (LCD) TVs, 22, 23

picture tubes, 20, 21
pixels, 19, 20, 21, 22, 23, 26
plasma TVs, 23

radio waves, 7, 8–9, 10, 11, 14, 15, 16, 17, 18, 24, 28
relay towers, 11, 12
remote controls, 24–25, 27, 28

satellites, 14, 15, 28
satellite TV, 11, 14–15, 18

TV cameras, 6–7
TV screens, 19, 20, 21, 22, 23, 26
TV signals
    analog, 16, 17
    audio, 7, 16
    digital, 16, 17, 18, 21
    video, 7, 16

Zworykin, Vladimir, 28